Cross Stitcher
MAGAZINE'S

Complete Introduction to
Cross Stitch

Wendy Gardiner

First published in 1995 by
Future Books
A division of Future Publishing Limited
30 Monmouth Street, Bath BA1 2BW

Cross stitch designs copyright © 1995
Text and photographs copyright © Future Publishing 1995

The moral right of the author has been asserted

Designed by Maria Bowers
Text by Wendy Gardiner
Edited by Kate John
Photographic styling by Lez Gardiner
Photography by Graham Cooper and Lez Gardiner

A CIP catalogue record of this book is
available from the British Library

ISBN: 1 85981 002 0

Printed and bound in Malaysia
by Times Offset (M) SDN BHD Group

2 4 6 8 10 9 7 5 3 1

We take great care to ensure that what we print is accurate, but
we cannot accept liability for any mistakes or misprints.

If you would like more information on our other stitching titles
please write to: The Publisher, Future Books at the above address

CONTENTS

KEY TO PROJECTS

TIME		DIFFICULTY	
	Less than a month.		Skilled
	Less than a week.		Intermediate
	An evening.		Beginner

FOREWORD

Cross Stitcher magazine's *Complete Introduction to Cross Stitch* has over 30 inspiring new ideas for the home, all beautifully photographed in full colour. The easy to follow step-by-step photography and clear charts make every project easily approachable, even for absolute beginners.

Choose from practical gifts that are easy to make, beautifully co-ordinated sets for kitchen or bedroom or commemorative designs to keep forever.

The informative 'Basics' section, accompanied by colourful photographs, explains essential information on materials and techniques to ensure perfect results every time.

chapter 1
THE BASICS

GETTING STARTED

SIMPLE CROSS STITCH

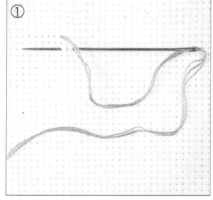

1. Step one – top left to bottom right.

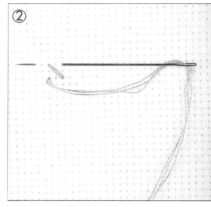

2. Step two – bottom left to top right.

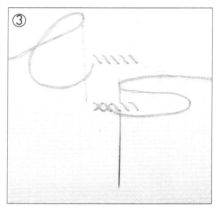

3. Work in rows in two stages. First, form lower cross then work back along the row to complete the upper cross.

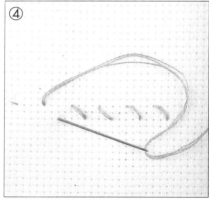

4. Work in rows in four stages. Firstly, work every other lower cross.

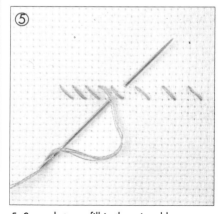

5. Second stage, fill in the missed lower cross on the same row.

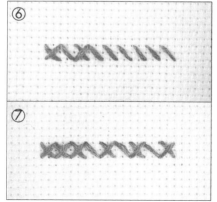

6. Thirdly, work along the row forming alternative top crosses.

7. Finally, form the remaining top crosses.

STITCHES

A cross stitch is simply one that is formed by two or more stitches crossing each other. The angle of the cross decides the type of cross stitch, which varies from a simple straight cross to, say, the more complicated interlaced Maltese Cross.

It is important to note that the top diagonal cross should always be worked in the same direction – unless an obvious light-shade effect is desired. Simple cross stitch can be worked in three basic ways.

When using canvas it is best to stitch each complete cross individually before proceeding to the next one. It is also essential that each cross stitch completely covers the canvas, so the thread choice is important.

The second method of working a cross stitch is to work a row. This is particularly suited to plain or evenweave fabric such as gingham. Simply work a line of diagonal stitches in one direction and then work back along the line in the opposite direction.

The third option, only suitable for evenweave fabrics, is a variation on the row method and is particularly useful when working a large design area. The lower row of diagonals is worked in two journeys and then the top row of diagonals is worked again in two journeys, each stitch completed alternately.

Other stitches used in conjunction with cross stitch for outlining or embroidery include:

Basting/Tacking Stitch

Used to mark the design area of holed fabrics together before sewing. The stitches are then removed once the design is complete. Use bold contrasting colour of thread so that it is easy to see.

Slip Stitch

To give an almost invisible finish on hems, facings etc. Use thread that matches the fabric for best results. Catch a strand or two of fabric, slide approximately 0.4cm along and up through the folded hem or facing. Catch another strand or two of main fabric, directly below and repeat to the end.

Running Stitch

Stitch in one direction along a complete line, leaving gaps between stitches. Return along the line, filling in the gaps to create an unbroken line using just one strand of thread.

Backstitch

Stitch each straight stitch individually when outlining a shape. Again, use only one strand of thread so that the outline does not dominate the design.

FABRICS

There are three main fabric categories for cross stitch designs; evenweave, plain weave and canvas.

Canvas

Canvas is made of vertical and horizontal threads woven together to produce precisely spaced holes between threads, resulting in a regular grid-like structure.

Canvas can be made from stiffened cotton, linen, silk gauze or plastic. It is commonly available in white or ecru. The two main types of canvas are single canvas and double canvas. The single version is formed by single vertical and horizontal threads whilst the double canvas, logically, has pairs of vertical and horizontal threads.

Canvas comes in a wide range of gauges (count). The count is the number of threads which can be stitched in 2.5cm (1in); for example, 11 HPI = holes per inch. Coarser count, say 3HPI – 5HPI is suitable for rugs.

Evenweave Fabric

Evenweave fabrics are particularly suited to basic Cross Stitch. They are, as the name suggests, made up by an equal quantity and thickness of vertical and horizontal threads, providing the same number of threads in a given area. Most popular evenweave fabrics are *Aida*, *Hardanger*, *Ainring* and *Glenshee*.

Aida has four threads woven together to form distinct blocks over which the stitches are formed, whilst *Hardangar* fabric has pairs of threads woven together.

The size of the stitches can be easily varied with evenweave fabric simply by working each stitch over more or less threads of the weave. For instance, a stitch worked over five threads of the evenweave will obviously be larger than one worked over three threads.

Plain Weave Fabrics

Plain weave fabrics can be difficult to use and only those with a regular woven or printed design, such as gingham, can be easily used for Cross Stitch. With these, the pattern in the fabric provides the necessary grid for working crossed stitches evenly and neatly and facilitates following a graph. Pitfalls to avoid are choosing too fine a fabric for the thread, which

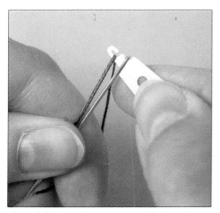

Thread the needle using a needle threader.

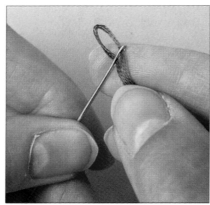

Slip the crisp loop through the eye of the needle.

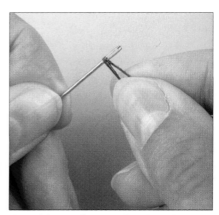

Thread the needle manually – loop the thread around the needle eye, pull firmly.

will result in a distorted or puckered background. It is also best to choose a fabric that is firmly woven and will allow the thread to be passed easily in and out.

THREADS

Embroidery threads come in a wide range of colours and weights. Some skeins of thread are multi-stranded and can be divided to create the thickness/weight

TIP

If you choose to use a different count canvas to that called for, remember that the finished piece will be a different size. A finer count (more stitches per inch) will produce a smaller piece whilst a coarser gauge will produce a larger piece.

required; others are twisted and must be used as one thread.

In this book, we have mostly used stranded thread. This is a loosely twisted thread, usually made up of six strands that is slightly shiny. The skeins can be separated into single strands and worked in any combination from one to six strands, depending on the project. Although the colour range is extremely extensive, it can be easily extended to create individual colours by mixing strands from different skeins.

Other threads that are suited to cross stitch include:
Pearl Cotton – a twisted 2-ply thread with high sheen that is used as supplied. **Soft Embroidery Cotton** – a 5-ply thread which is fairly thick and has a matt finish. Generally it is used as a single thread on heavier fabrics.
Stranded Pure Silk – a 7-ply, shiny thread that can be divided. Whilst many brilliant colours are available, silk is more difficult than cotton to work with and does need

to be dry-cleaned. **Tapestry Wool** – a tightly twisted 4-ply wool – used on coarse canvas for rugs etc.

FRAMES

There are two basic types of frame; ring and roller frames. Frames are used to keep the fabric taut whilst working on the design, which will prevent distortion and puckering, as well as help keep stitches even.

The ring frames, available in a variety of sizes are made from two rings. The fabric is laid between the two, which are then tightened by a screw holding the fabric firmly

Divide stranded cotton and use two or three threads at a time.

Suitable fabrics for cross stitching.

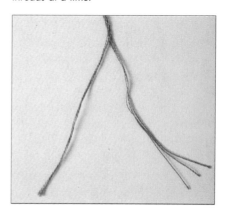

in place.

However, if marks are left by the ring, they can be difficult to remove. Therefore, it is advisable to ensure that the completed design is well within the frame. To avoid marks, bind the inner ring with tissue or fabric.

The roller frame is used primarily for large pieces of work. The fabric or canvas is tacked to the top and bottom rollers and then laced to the sides to hold taut.

OTHER EQUIPMENT

Whilst it is not essential to have other specific equipment to complete any cross stitch design, there are many items available that are a great help. The usual sewing accessories such as, a fine pair of embroidery scissors; tape measure, sharp glass-headed pins; choice of needles; pin cushion and sewing machine can be complemented by other specialist aids, designed to simplify work and make it more enjoyable.

These aids include such items as a *Needle Threader*, particularly one that copes with thicker thread; *Project Cards* to hold threads for

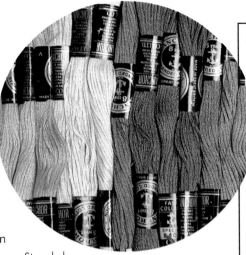

Stranded cotton.

easy identification and *Needleholder Cards* with magnetic strips to hold threaded needles – particularly useful for designs with many colour changes. *Magnetic Boards* with magnetic strips will hold graphs in place whilst a *Line Magnifier* will help amplify small or complex graphs. Alternatively a magnifier that hangs from the neck and props against the body is a great way to keep both hands free for handling the work, whilst enlarging the area to be worked on. Finally, a *Project Carrying Case*, with ample pockets for threads, haberdashery and projects will keep everything together.

USEFUL TIPS

1 Thread – use thread in lengths of approximately 40cm (15¾in) to avoid tangling. Longer threads also have a tendency to fray and can lose their natural sheen if over handled.

2 Starting and Finishing – avoid using knots as these may well show through or cause a lump. Instead use 2-3 tiny back stitches in a space that will later be covered by stitches.
Alternatively, leave a tail (approximately 5cm/2in)) which can be darned in later. When finishing, slide the needle through a row of stitches, approximately 3cm (1¼in) long, before cutting off the loose end.

3 Frames – bind the inner round frames in a length of cotton tape to help prevent marking and/or damage to fabric. Secure with masking tape.

4 Fabric – prevent edges fraying whilst working by running a line of machine stitching around the edges. Also allow at least 12cm (5in) extra for work that will be framed and 7cm (3in) for all unframed pieces.

5 Transferring Designs to Fabric – when working from a chart on evenweave fabric or canvas, simply follow the chart by counting the threads to determine where to position the stitch. With plain weave fabrics you might prefer to trace the design onto the fabric or tack it in place.

6 Basting/Tacking – it is advisable to plot with tacking stitches the area to be worked – the centre, borders, and corners etc.

A selection of sewing aids.

Frames and mounts for cross stitch designs.

ALPHABET

STITCHING INSTRUCTIONS

The very nature of cross stitch epitomises handcrafted gifts and treasured mementoes. It is therefore a good idea when starting cross stitch to practice simple numbers and an alphabet. We have chosen an evenweave 11HPI pearl aida and DMC stranded cotton. The 11HPI aida is ideal for medium size cross stitch and simple designs whilst the six strand thread can be divided into single strands to suit the needs of the various projects. Generally, three strands of stranded cotton will produce an even, fully covered area.

These will always be useful for a variety of projects, and can later be incorporated into many other personalised designs.

STITCHING THE ALPHABET

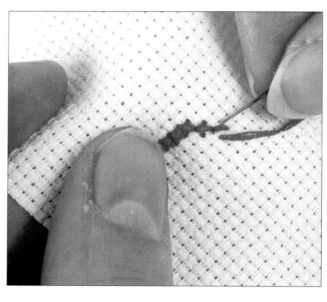

1 Starting from the back, secure the thread and then pull the needle through to the front. Sew each cross stitch individually, starting each stitch at the same point each time – ie: bottom left over to top right, under to bottom right, over to top left, under to bottom left of next etc.

3 When planning the motto or text for a personalised memento, remember to bear in mind the varying heights and width of each letter/number used. Calculate the number of holes each requires, plus spaces between letters and words. The simplest method is to write on a piece of graph paper, using each square as a stitch with each of the intersections of the ruled lines as one hole.

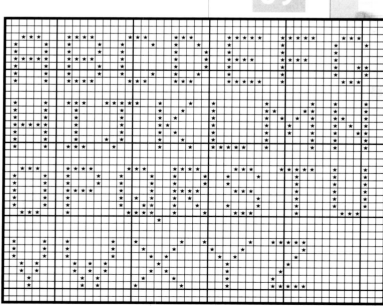

1234567890

ABCDEFG
HIJKLMN
OPQRSTU
VWXYZ

abcdefghi
jklmnopqr
stuvwxy
z

2 Each letter or number is counted over a specific number of holes. For instance, when using lower case letters remember that some will have ascenders and descenders that will need to be higher or deeper than those without, so extra space between rows of text are necessary. Equally, letters that are wider, such as M or W will take up more space horizontally than others.

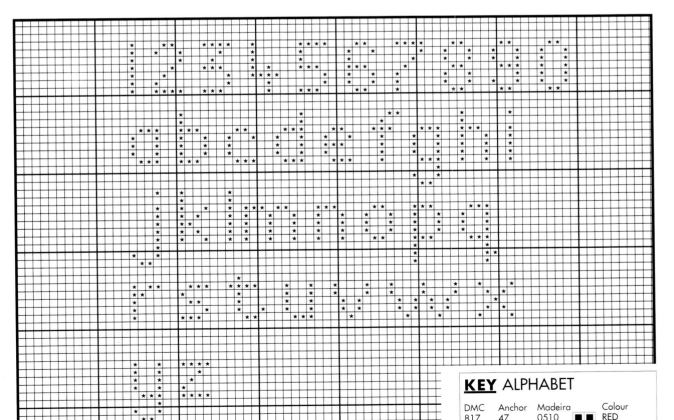

PENCIL CASE

Create this brightly coloured, personalised accessory for children, to fill with their favourite pencils and pens.

STITCHING INSTRUCTIONS

KEY PENCIL CASE

DMC	Anchor	Madeira		Colour
820	139	0904	⊙ ⊙	BLUE
543	372	2013	● ●	CREAM

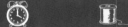

MAKING THE PENCIL CASE

1 Using a nice bright red 14HPI aida, cut a piece approximately 23 x 26cm (9 x 10in). Mark the area in which the lettering is to go – the top line approximately 6cm from top fabric edge. Allow at least 9 clear holes between lines of lettering. Then, start lettering, approximately 4cm from the left edge, using three strands of embroidery thread.

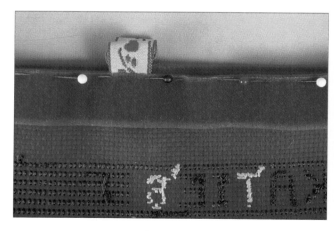

4 Turn raw edges in approximately 20cm (7in) at top and bottom. Cut velcro to fit along these edges, which will form the opening, and pin in place. At the same time, add small ribbon loops sandwiched between raw edge and velcro back. Baste and then machine stitch velcro to turned edge along the outer edge, ensuring you catch the ribbon loops as you go.

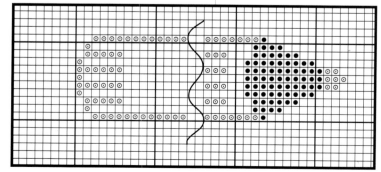

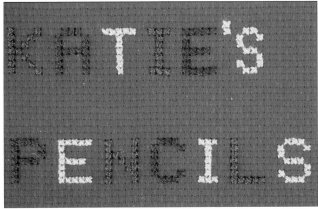

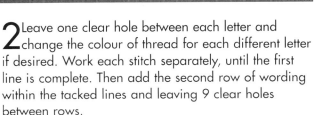

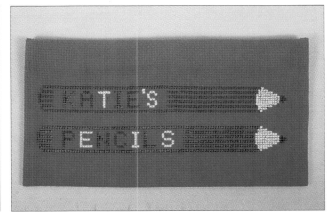

2 Leave one clear hole between each letter and change the colour of thread for each different letter if desired. Work each stitch separately, until the first line is complete. Then add the second row of wording within the tacked lines and leaving 9 clear holes between rows.

3 Following the chart, cross stitch the pencils around the two rows of wording, using three strands of thread. The pencil end should start approximately 2cm from the left edge, finishing with the pencil tip approximately 2.5cm (1in) from right edge. Fold the aida in half lengthways to check the design is nicely centred before turning, right sides together, ready to sew.

5 Fold the aida in half, with right sides together, and top velcro edges matching. Then machine stitch approximately 1cm from the selvage. Overlook the stitched seams to secure firmly and prevent fraying. Turn to right side and press, using a dry press cloth and warm iron.

BOOK MARKS

A stylish addition to any good book.

STITCHING INSTRUCTIONS

KEY BOOK MARKS

DMC	Anchor	Madeira			Colour
957	50	0613	●	●	PINK
326	47	0509	×	×	RED

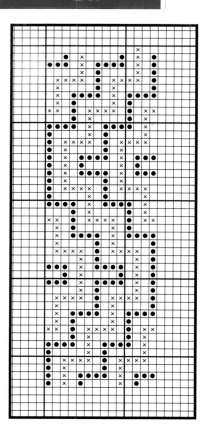

MAKING THE BOOKMARKS

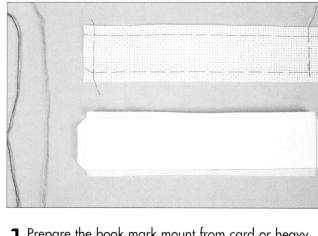

1 Prepare the book mark mount from card or heavy weight paper, cutting a piece approximately 5cm wide x 18cm (2 x 7in) in length. Score border approximately 0.7cm wide around the edge, trimming the four corners off so that when folded over, they will mitre neatly. Using 14 HPI fabric, cut a piece approximately 7 x 21cm (2¾ x 8¼in). Tack stitch around the outer edge of the design area.

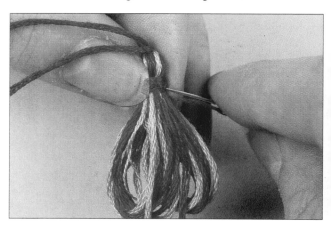

4 To make a co-ordinating tassel, simply wrap full strands of both colours around two fingers about six times. Holding one end firmly between thumb and fingers, stitch through the other end and then wrap the thread around the neck of the tassel until it is firmly bound together. Leave two long ends to secure the bookmark. Cut through the loops at the loose end, separating the strands with a pin to fan out.

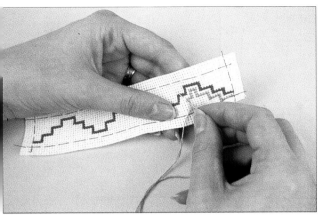

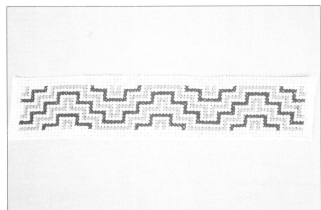

2 Start the design in the main colour, following the chart. When the centre of the design is reached, simply reverse the pattern to complete the other half of the design. Next, using the second colour, work another row of the design. Any design can be used from names to pictures although simple geometric designs are easier to follow.

3 Fill in the remainder of the design area, using three strands of stranded cotton and working each colour alternatively until complete. A third colour could be added to completely cover the background if desired. Remove the tacking stitch border and then trim the finished piece to approximately 3.5 x 16.5cm (1 3/8 x 6 1/2 in).

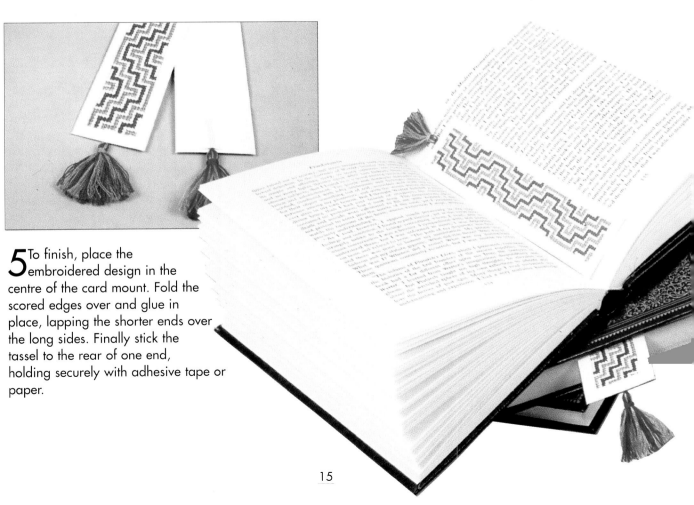

5 To finish, place the embroidered design in the centre of the card mount. Fold the scored edges over and glue in place, lapping the shorter ends over the long sides. Finally stick the tassel to the rear of one end, holding securely with adhesive tape or paper.

CAKE FRILLS

Impress your family and friends with this festive stitching.

STITCHING INSTRUCTIONS

MAKING THE CAKE FRILLS

KEY CAKE FRILLS					
DMC	**Anchor**	**Madeira**			**Colour**
817	19	0211	#	#	RED
890	879	1314	●	●	GREEN
743	302	018	ς	ς	YELLOW

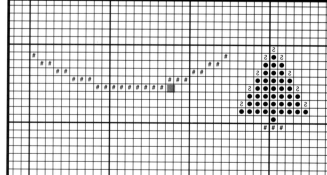

16

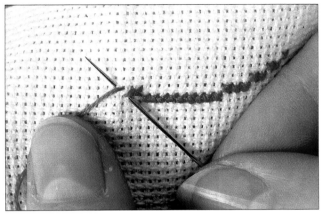

1 Cut a piece of 5cm wide 16HPI trim to fit snugly around your Christmas cake adding 4cm for seam allowances. (If cake size is not known, err on the generous side as any excess can always be overlapped.) Working with two strands of bright red embroidery thread and following the chart, begin the first garland 8 holes from top edge.

2 Leave 9 holes between garlands for the Christmas Tree. Again, following chart, cross stitch the tree using two strands of deep green embroidery thread. Finish each tree with a bright red base to match the garlands. Then add a row of candles using just one strand of thread. Work a cross stitch candle to alternate rows on either side of the tree and all three top rows.

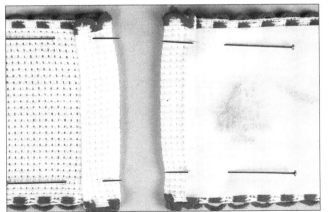

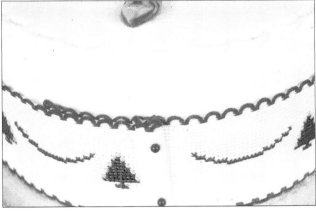

3 On the underside of the cake frill, turn in the ends once approximately 1cm and then again to encase the raw edges. Pin in place. Cut a piece of greaseproof paper to the finished length to fit within the trim edges, say 4.5cm (1¾in) wide. Attach a cake frill with tiny stitches at intervals to hold in place.

4 Once the cake icing is set, add the embroidered cake frill, joining the ends at the back of the cake. If necessary, overlap the frill to fit snugly around the cake. Pin in place, preferably with glass headed pins that are easy to remove.

SAMPLER

Stitch this delightfully traditional sampler to celebrate a special occasion, or to be enjoyed as a lasting memento.

STITCHING INSTRUCTIONS

KEY SAMPLER

DMC	Anchor	Madeira		Colour
814	70	0601	● ●	BURGUNDY
605	74	0607	J J	PINK
414	273	1801	× ×	GREY
605	74	0607	☐ ☐	PINK

18 & ROSETTE

414	273	1801	× ×	GREY
605	74	0607	J J	PINK
814	70	0601	● ●	BURGUNDY

KEYS & BORDER

605	74	0607	J J	PINK
814	70	0601	● ●	BURGUNDY

MAKING THE SAMPLER

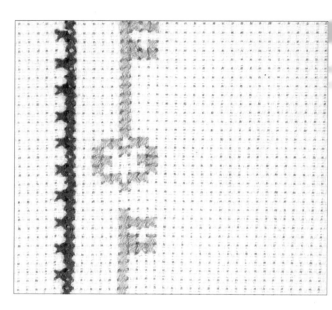

1 Cut the 11HPI pearl aida to approximately 40cm (15 ¾in) square and mark the outer edge of the design area with a tacking stitch. Begin the border design seven holes from the edge, following the chart. Work around the whole edge using 3 strands of burgundy thread for the border. Leave one clear hole between border and key motif and then complete the line of keys using pale pink cotton.

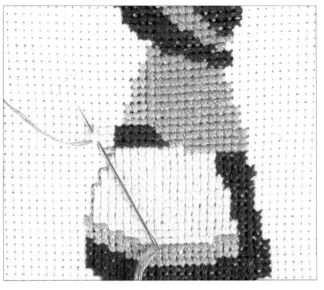

2 Once the design and motto has been completed, back stitch an outline around the edge of the little girl's pinafore and hand, using a single strand of the role pink thread. In this project, an 18th birthday has been highlighted in silver to contrast with the pinks. Use the alphabet and numerical charts on page 10 to personalise your own design.

3 Once the sampler is completed, cut a piece of card approximately 25.5cm (10in) square. Centre the design carefully over the card, folding the excess fabric to the back (approximately 5cm/2in all around – trim any excess away). Hold in place temporarily with dabs of tape and then lace the back over the card, using strong mercerised cotton. Pull the aida taut to hold securely in place and then fasten off.

4 Slip the finished sampler into a suitable frame, staining the wood to match if preferred. Add another piece of card as backing, cutting the size to fit snugly in the frame. Hold in place with heavy duty tape. Finally, add a hanging hook to the back, again using heavy duty tape to secure firmly.

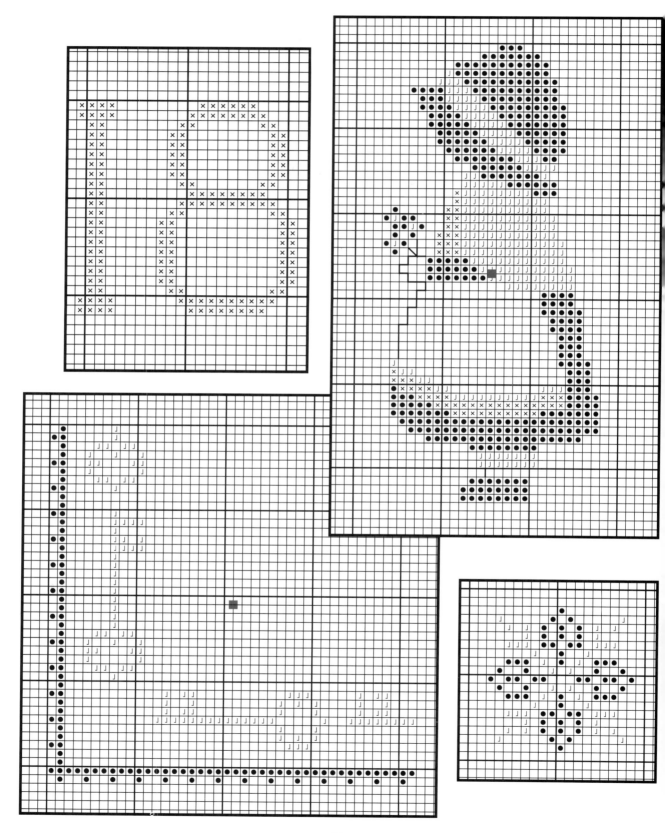

chapter 2
HOME
DECORATING
IDEAS

TOWEL TREATMENT

This flower design will add an appliquéd flair to your towels.

STITCHING INSTRUCTIONS

KEY TOWEL

DMC	Anchor	Madeira			Colour
437	368	2011	×	×	BEIGE
327	100	0714	◖	◖	VIOLET
701	227	1305	♥	♥	GREEN
743	302	0108	●	●	YELLOW
219	108	0802	⊙	⊙	MAUVE

MAKING UP THE TOWEL

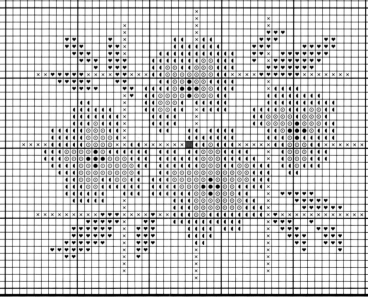

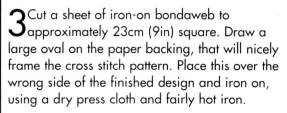 **3** Cut a sheet of iron-on bondaweb to approximately 23cm (9in) square. Draw a large oval on the paper backing, that will nicely frame the cross stitch pattern. Place this over the wrong side of the finished design and iron on, using a dry press cloth and fairly hot iron.

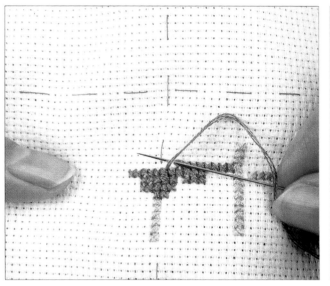

1 Cut a 23cm (9in) square of 14HPI aida and tack the edges to prevent them from fraying. Mark the centre, using two rows of long running stitches. Begin the design at a convenient point, working each stitch individually using DMC cotton perle and following the chart.

2 Continue working the design, following the chart. When changing colour, avoid trailing threads across the back of the work as they may show through, instead, tie off each flower or trellis and start again.

4 Holding the stiffened design in one hand, cut out around the oval shape. The bondaweb will prevent the aida edges from fraying. Place the oval onto a towel at the centre of one end.

5 Secure the oval in place using a warm iron and dry press cloth. Press firmly to make the bondaweb adhesive stick. Finally, machine stitch the oval edges to the towel, using a tight zigzag or overlocking stitch.

FRAME FAVOURITES

Dress up a frame for a favourite portrait.

STITCHING INSTRUCTIONS

KEY FRAME

DMC	Anchor	Madeira		Colour
3818	218	1405	● ●	DARK GREEN
471	265	1603	◖ ◖	PALE GREEN
718	88	0706	♥ ♥	DARK PINK
604	51	0614	· ·	PALE PINK

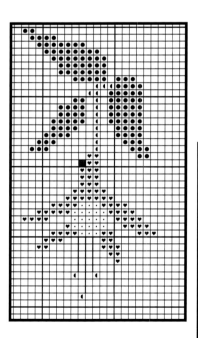

MAKING THE FRAME

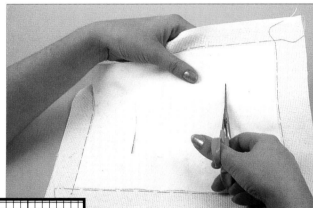

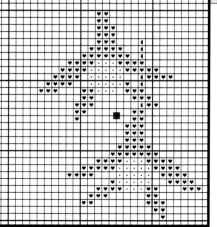

3 Cut a piece of cotton poplin to line the frame – it should be just within the frame dimensions. Machine stitch to right side of aida along the picture (inner) edge running stitch, pivoting at the corners. Remove the tacking stitches and trim centre piece approximately 0.5cm from the stitching.

1 Prepare the picture frame components – using mounting card for the backing, strut and frame front. Cut the back and front pieces approximately 19 x 22cm (7½ x 8¾ in). Cut out the picture area, approximately 10.5 x 13.5cm (4⅛ x 5¼ in) and glue some wadding to the front piece to provide padding. Cover the back with cotton poplin.

2 Cut a piece of 11HPI aida approximately 24 x 29cm (9¼ x 11½ in). Mark the front frame section and picture area, approximately 10.5 x 13.5cm (4⅛ x 5¼ in) with running stitches. Following the chart, cross stitch two overlapping fuchsia in one corner and a group of leaves in the opposite corner, using DMC cotton perle.

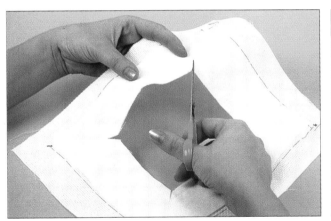

4 Once the centre pieces have been trimmed away, clip the corners diagonally to within 1mm of stitching. Turn the lining to wrong side, folding along the stitching line. Pin and press to form a crisp edge. Insert the padded card, prepared earlier. Fold the outer edges of aida over the card, lap with the lining and glue in place.

5 Glue the covered back to front at three sides, leaving the top open to insert photograph. Score across the strut approximately 2.5cm (1in) from narrow end and then cover the strut with cotton poplin. With double-sided tape or glue, stick the strut to the back of the frame, ensuring the bottom of frame and strut are equal.

FUCHSIA INSPIRED LAMPSHADE

Brighten up your lampshade with this colourful fuchsia design.

STITCHING INSTRUCTIONS

KEY LAMPSHADE

DMC	Anchor	Madeira			Colour
3818	218	1405	●	●	DARK GREEN
471	265	1603	◖	◖	PALE GREEN
718	88	0706	♥	♥	DARK PINK
604	51	0614	·	·	PALE PINK

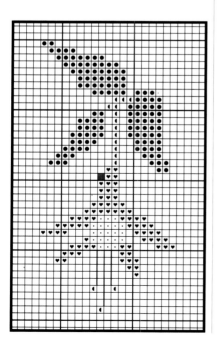

MAKING THE LAMPSHADE

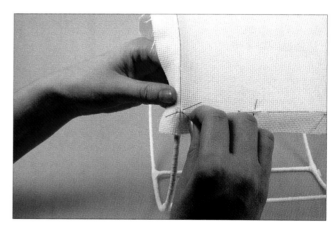

3 Pin the aida to the taped frame along the running stitches. Hand stitch to the frame, folding in the 1cm seam allowance of the aida at the top and bottom of the frame. Overlap the two side edges, turning the raw edge of the top piece under and then hand stitch to the frame through both edges.

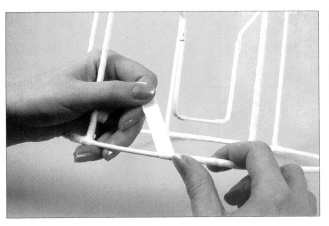

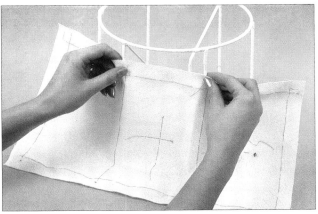

1 Using cotton bias binding, bind your chosen lampshade frame, wrapping the tape around each part very tightly. Secure with one or two stitches where each vertical pole meets the top and bottom of the frame.

2 Cut two pieces of 11HPI aida approximately 2cm deeper and wider than half of the frame. Using contrasting thread and large running stitches, mark the frame dimensions and panels on the aida. In addition, mark the centre of each panel. Cross stitch a single fuchsia in each panel, following the chart.

4 Add the braid along the top edge of the frame, either by gluing in place or by hand stitching. Also cover the side seams with a line of braid, again either glued or stitched in place.

5 Glue the fringing around the bottom edge of the lampshade, so that the fringing hangs down. Finally, add the braid trim over the fringing to match the top and side braiding. Again glue or stitch in place.

DECORATIVE CUSHION

A delightful cushion, the design of which is both delicate and stylish in detail.

STITCHING INSTRUCTIONS

KEY CUSHION

DMC	Anchor	Madeira		Colour
3818	218	1405	● ●	DARK GREEN
471	265	1603	◖ ◖	PALE GREEN
718	88	0706	♥ ♥	DARK PINK
604	51	0614	· ·	PALE PINK

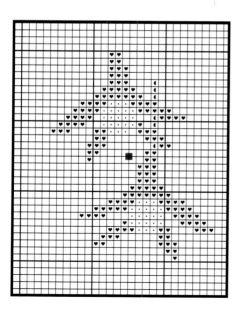

MAKING THE CUSHION

1 Cut a small piece of 11HPI aida approximately 16cm (6¼in) square. Mark the centre using a contrasting thread and two lines of long running stitches. Following the chart and using DMC cotton perle, cross stitch the overlapping fuchsias.

4 To make the cushion cover, simply cut two fabric squares approximately 2cm larger than the cushion. Add the lace trimmed panel to the centre of one cover piece, either using bondaweb or machine stitching around the edges. Sandwich *embroidery anglais* edging between right sides of cover and stitch three sides of the cushion. Turn and press. Insert cushion, slip stitch remaining edge and trim together.

2 Cut two lengths of ribbon threaded lace trim approximately 32cm (12½in) long – to fit around the cross stitch panel. Prepare the corners by folding lace trim in two and machine stitching diagonally across the folded corner. Trim away the corner piece 0.5cm from stitching. Press seam edges open.

3 Pin two lace trims to the right side of the cross stitch panel forming a square frame. Overlap two corners and stitch together. Machine stitch trim to panel either side of the ribbon, pivoting at the corners.

PILLOWSLIP EDGING

Transform your bedlinen with this refreshing fuchsia and trellis design.

STITCHING INSTRUCTIONS

KEY PILLOWSLIP EDGING

DMC	Anchor	Madeira			Colour
3818	218	1405	●	●	DARK GREEN
471	265	1603	◖	◖	PALE GREEN
718	88	0706	♥	♥	DARK PINK
604	51	0614	·	·	PALE PINK
TRELLIS					
437	368	2011	●	●	BEIGE

STITCHING THE EDGING

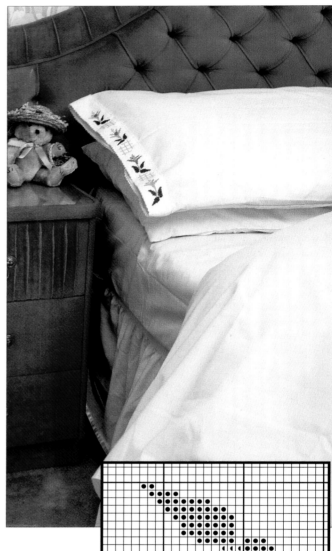

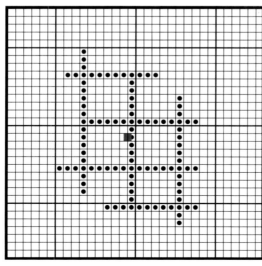

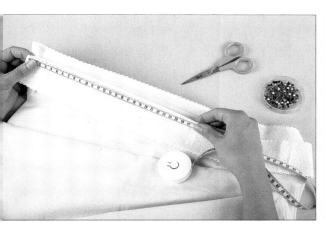

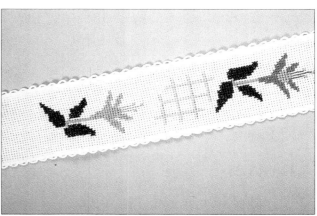

1 To complete the bedroom set of lampshade, cushion and picture frame, add co-ordinating bedlinen. Measure around the pillow slip opening, adding 4cm (1½in) seam allowance. Then, cut a piece of 5cm (2in) wide trimmed embroidery fabric to the correct length.

2 Divide the strip in half and starting from one end, cross stitch single fuchsias, alternating the colour of the flowers and using DMC cotton perle. Allow 28 holes, approximately 4cm (1½in) between each flower in which to add a trellis, again using DMC cotton perle.

3 At the halfway point along the fabric, change direction and cross stitch the fuchsias facing the opposite way. Once completed, pin the trim to the pillowslip edge, turning the raw edges under 2cm at each end. Machine stitch in place along both sides. Add the same trim to the top sheet edge for a complete set.

4 For the top sheet, measure the width of the sheet, adding 4cm (1½in) for seam allowance. Then cut this length of embroidery trim and embroider the fuchsias and trellis alternating the shades of the flowers as you go. Machine stitch to the underside of the sheet so that when folded down, it will be on the top edge, so complementing the pillowcase design.

BUTTERFLY NAPKIN SET

A pastoral design to add a sophisticated touch to the dining table or a bit of style to a summer's picnic.

STITCHING INSTRUCTIONS

KEY NAPKINS

DMC	Anchor	Madeira		Colour
310	403	BLACK	■ ■	BLACK
554	108	802	O O	MAUVE
895	683	1314	◄ ◄	DARK GREEN
743	305	0109	J J	YELLOW
522	261	1513	▲ ▲	PALE GREEN
310	403	BLACK	☐	BLACK

STITCHING THE NAPKINS

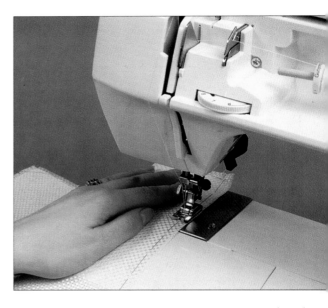

1 Cut a 30cm (11in) square at 11HPI Damask aida to match the table cloth. Tack around the square approximately 0.5cm from the edges using thread to match the fabric. Machine stitch along the tacking lines.

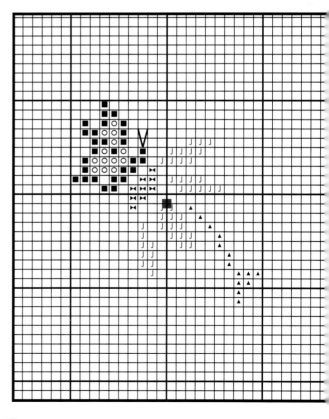

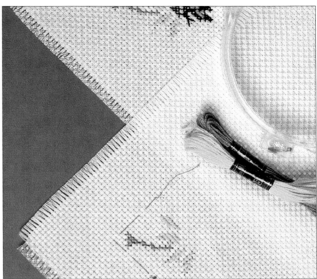

2 Gently pull the cloth threads from edges to create the fringe. Work each side separately, until the line of machine stitching is reached. Remove the tacking stitches before marking the corner to be embroidered, approximately 15 holes – 5cm (2in) – from one corner.

3 Following the chart, and using three strands of DMC stranded embroidery thread, start the stem at the corner. Complete with the butterfly, adding antennaes and French knots to finish (see the table cloth project overleaf, for French knot instructions).

MATCHING TABLE CLOTH

This matching cloth, together with the napkin set, makes a winning combination for creating a fresh table decoration.

STITCHING INSTRUCTIONS

KEY TABLE CLOTH

DMC	Anchor	Madeira		Colour
522	261	1513	J J	PALE GREEN
895	683	1314	× ×	DARK GREEN
310	403	BLACK	■ ■	BLACK
554	108	0802	⊙ ⊙	MAUVE
792	941	0914	► ►	BLUE
743	305	0109	∩ ∩	YELLOW
310	403	BLACK		BLACK

STITCHING THE TABLE CLOTH

1 To make a table cloth, use a wide fabric available by the metre, such as DMC's 11HPI Damask aida. For a rectangular or oval table, cut a piece approximately 65cm (26in) longer than the table. For a small circular table, cut a square of fabric. Prepare fabric edges for fringing by tacking and then machine stitching approximately 1cm from selvage.

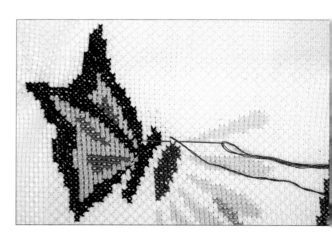

4 Continue the design, working each stitch individually. When changing colours, avoid trailing threads across the back of the work as they may snag or show through. Start again, weaving tail ends in as you go. Finish the butterfly with antennae made from two long stitches topped with French knots.

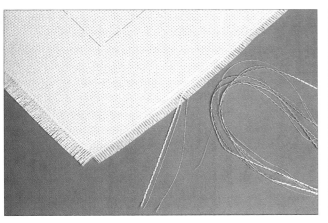

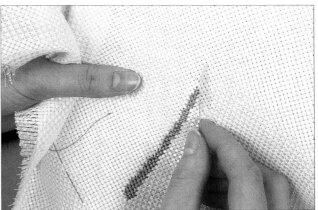

2 Fringe the edges by gently pulling threads away, until the line of machine stitching is reached. Work with two or three threads at a time and complete each side before starting the next. Tack marking lines approximately 12cm (4¾in) from each corner as guidelines for the cross stitch design.

3 Using three strands of embroidery thread, start the stem of the flower design at a point 11 holes – 4cm (1½in) – from the corner guidelines. Follow the chart for the flower and butterfly. To co-ordinate with your own dinner service, simply change the colours of the flower and butterfly to suit.

5 To make a French knot, start with the thread on the right side, hold thread firmly and wrap around the needle two or three times. Still holding the thread, insert needle close to the point it originally came from and pull through to the rear. The knot will stay in place.

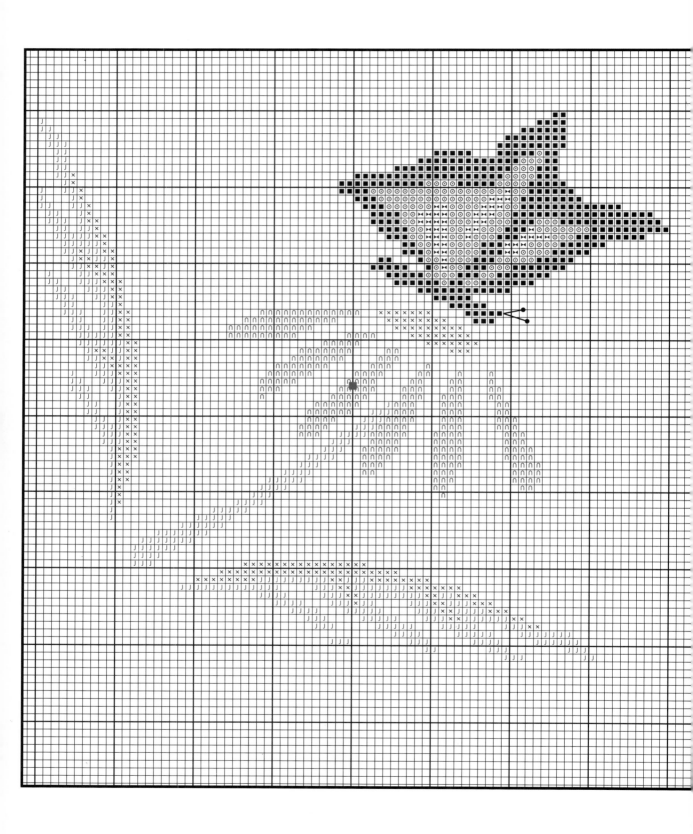

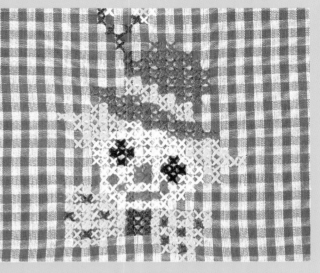

chapter 3
CHILDREN

Stephen

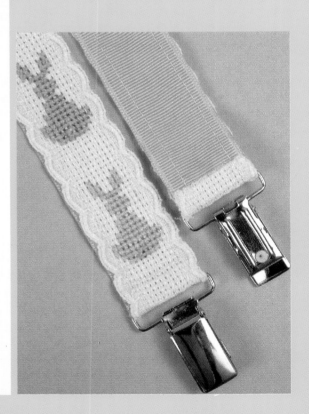

ADVENT CALENDAR

Count the days before Christmas in this great tradition - by stitching this festive wall-hanging, which will thrill children and adults alike!

STITCHING INSTRUCTIONS

KEY ADVENT CALENDAR

DMC	Anchor	Madeira		Colour
WHITE	1	WHITE	· ·	WHITE
310	BLACK	BLACK	■ ■	BLACK
971	316	0204	★ ★	ORANGE

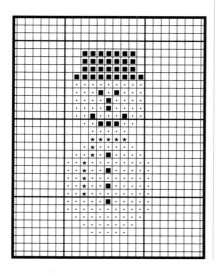

MAKING THE CALENDAR

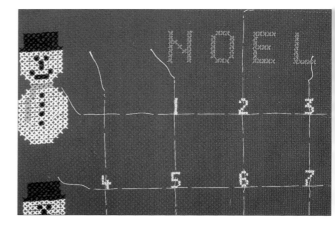

1 Cut a piece of bright red 14 HPI aida approximately 43cm wide x 54cm (17 x 21in) and machine stitch edges to prevent fraying. Using large running stitches, divide the fabric centre into 24 evenly spaced squares. With the 24th day at the foot, cross stitch each date on the relevant cross-piece of running stitches. Follow the chart to add four snowmen to either side, starting approximately 7cm (2¾ in) from the top edge and 4cm (1½ in) from the side.

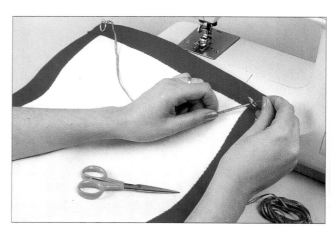

3 Machine stitch top approximately 2cm from edge to form a casing for a bamboo rod. Next add two curtain rings, one at either side, from which to hang the calendar. Alternatively, tie ribbon to the rings in order to form a pretty ribbon hanging.

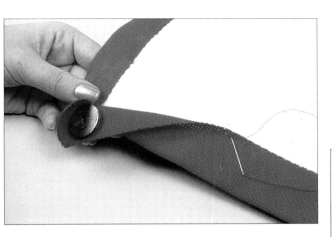

2 Add the wording as desired, centred over the dates by counting the number of letters/stitches to be used, halve the total and count back from the centre to find start point. Once complete, cut a piece of heavyweight interfacing to approximately 35 x 48cm (13 x 19in) to form backing. Turn edges of aida over and slip stitch in place, adding weight to bottom corners if desired.

4 Using a further 24 curtain rings, add one to each of the cross stitched dates. Sew firmly in place just below the numbers, centrally when below double figures. Make up 24 little parcels, wrapping some in paper or netting to vary the choice.

5 Hang the little gifts, one to each ring, varying the selection and size for an even balance.

PINAFORE BIB

Create this novelty dress in a few simple steps.

STITCHING INSTRUCTIONS

KEY CLOWN FACE

DMC	Anchor	Madeira		Colour
11	WHITE	1	☐ ☐	WHITE
742	303	0107	2 2	YELLOW
718	89	0707	● ●	PURPLE
797	123	0912	■ ■	BLUE
666	9046	0510	# #	RED
909	229	1303	○ ○	GREEN

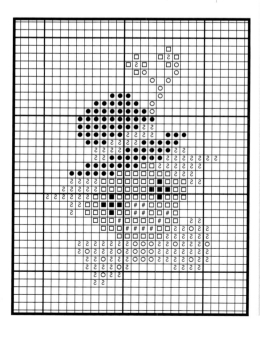

MAKING THE PINAFORE BIB

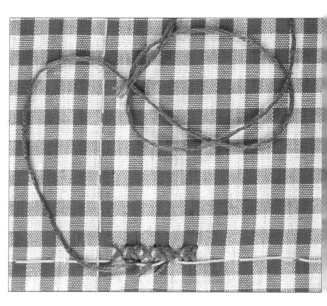

1 Cut a piece of gingham approximately 17 x 20cm (6¾ x 7¾in) which allows 3cm excess for easier handling. Mark the centre of the gingham, using long tacking stitches to define the design area. Using two strands of embroidery thread, begin the design.

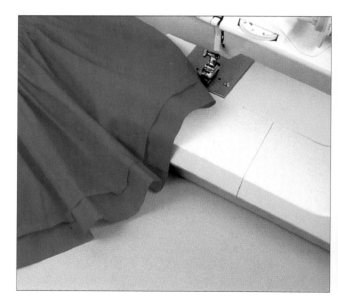

4 Make the trousers to complete the dungarees. Use a toddler's pattern and add elasticated cuffs. Alternatively, cuffs could be hemmed and turn up to show underside of denim. Make two buttonholes in ends of each strap.

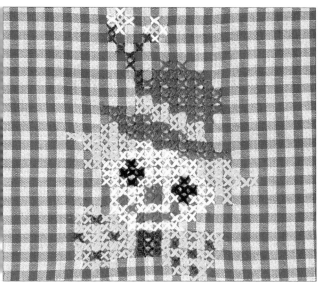

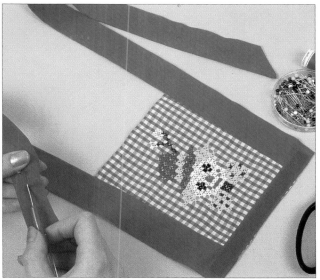

2 Following the chart, complete the motif, stitching four cross-stitches in each large gingham check. Once complete, trim the gingham to approximately 13 x 16cm (5 x 6⅜in). Add a denim backing, cut to the same size and machine stitch to gingham at top and bottom (right sides together). Turn and press.

3 Add the two straps, approximately 66cm (26in) long in matching denim. Fold in half and stitch one end and long edge, leaving last 16cm (6⅜in) open. Turn to right sides. Attach right side of unsewn strap end to right side of bib, stitch across end and side. Fold remaining strap edge back over to encase bib edge and slip stitch to finish.

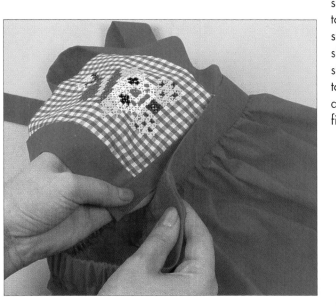

5 Add four poppas to inside waistband front and along bottom edge of bib, matching the positions. To join together, simply pop in place. Use the female sides of the poppa on trousers so that the stud will not press against body if bib is not worn. Finally, add buttons to back waistband.

DUNGAREE BIB

This bold bus design is a fun addition to any child's wardrobe.

STITCHING INSTRUCTIONS

KEY DUNGAREE BIB

DMC	Anchor	Madeira			Colour
666	9046	0510	#	#	RED
973	297	0105	·	·	YELLOW
WHITE	1	WHITE	□	□	WHITE
310	403	BLACK	■	■	BLACK

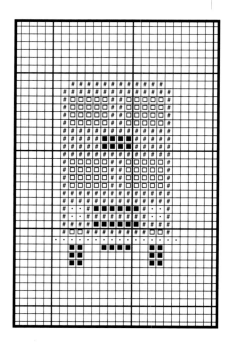

MAKING THE DUNGAREE BIB

1 As with the little pinafore, cut a piece of gingham approximately 17 x 20cm (6¾ x 7¾in) which allows 3cm excess for handling. Mark the centre of the gingham, using long tacking stitches to define the design area. Using two strands of embroidery thread, begin the design.

4 Make the trousers to complete the dungarees. Use a toddler's pattern and add elasticated cuffs. Alternatively, cuffs could be hemmed and turn up to show underside of denim. Make two buttonholes in ends of each strap.

2 Following the chart, complete the motif, stitching four cross-stitches in each large gingham check. Once complete, trim the gingham to approximately 13 x 16cm (5 x 6⅜in). Add a denim backing, cut to the same size and machine stitch to gingham at top and bottom (right sides together). Turn and press.

3 Add the two straps, approximately 66cm (26in) long in matching denim. Fold in half and stitch one end and long edge, leaving last 16cm (6⅜in) open. Turn to right sides. Attach right side of unsewn strap end to right side of bib, stitch across end and side. Fold remaining strap edge back over to encase bib edge and slip stitch to finish.

5 Add four poppas to inside waistband front and along bottom edge of bib, matching the positions. To join together, simply pop in place. Use the female sides of the poppa on trousers so that the stud will not press against body if bib is not worn. Finally, add buttons to back waistband.

HAIRBAND AND BRACES

Matching accessories that add individual style to an outfit.

KEY HAIRBAND AND BRACES

DMC	Anchor	Madeira			Colour
954	241	1212	●	●	GREEN
927	399	1802	■	■	GREY
605	25	0613	⊙	⊙	PINK

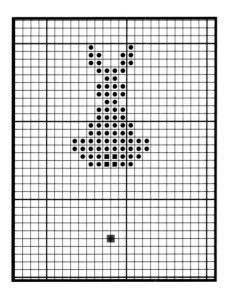

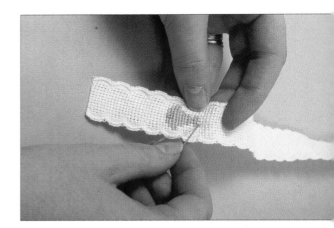

1 Using 0.25cm wide trim, cut a piece approximately 37.5cm (14¾ in) in length for the headband. Start the cross stitch design following the chart, approximately 4.5cm (1¾ in) from one raw edge. Begin with three strands of silver grey thread and cross stitch the bunny tail in the centre. Next, change to three strands of pink to complete the bunny design.

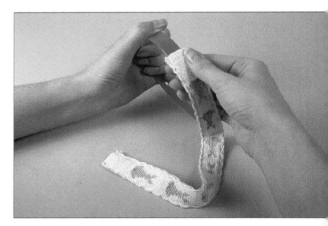

4 Feed the tube onto a child's hairband, working the design around to cover the full length. Work the braces in the same way, making each brace approximately 70cm (27½ in) long. Finish both ends with brace clips.

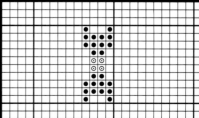

MAKING THE HAIRBAND AND BRACES

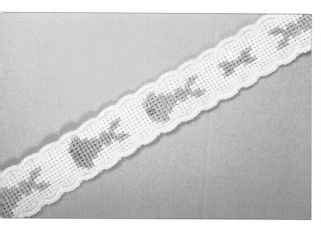

2 Start the next bunny, leaving 8 holes clear between each one, using pale green for the second body, changing back to pink for the third. Next, leave 5 holes before starting the centre bow design, using green for the bow and pink for the knot. Again leaving 5 holes clear, work three more bunnies with heads towards the centre and tails to the end, alternating pink and green for the bodies.

3 Cut a piece of 0.25cm wide grograin ribbon to the same length as the embroidered trim. Pin and then tack the two lengths, wrong sides together, turning in the short ends approximately 0.5cm to neaten. Machine stitch the two sides forming an open-ended tube.

BIRTHDAY PICTURE

Choose a child's favourite character for the perfect birthday design.

STITCHING INSTRUCTIONS

KEY TRAIN

DMC	Anchor	Madeira			Colour
318	399	1802	◆	◆	GREY
413	236	1713	◀	◀	DARK GREY
666	9046	0510	#	#	RED
972	303	0107	·	·	YELLOW
820	134	0913	●	●	ROYAL BLUE
WHIITE	1	WHITE	□	□	WHITE
762	234	1803	⊙	⊙	PALE GREY
310	403	BLACK	■	■	BLACK

MAKING THE BIRTHDAY PICTURE

3 Once the design is complete, stitch the train's face using just one strand of thread and backstitch for the eyes, nose and mouth. If a different design is preferred for a girl, substitute the house chart (page 78) or clown face (page 40). Start the design roughly in the middle, at the centre of the running stitches.

TIP
Use alphabet and numerical charts for name and dates, page 11.

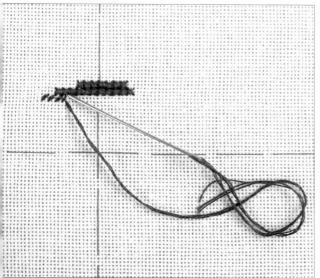

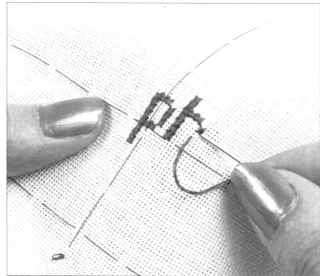

1 Using very fine evenweave embroidery linen, cut a piece 26 x 34cm (10 x 13in). Tack the edge and mark the centre with large running stitches. Follow the chart, and using three strands of DMC embroidery thread, begin the design working in short rows. Again with running stitches, mark the position of the two lines of wording (approximately 3cm/1¼in apart).

2 To centre the wording within the picture, work out how many stitches (and spaces) are required for the name and date, halve the total and then start the cross stitch at this halfway point, at the centre of the running stitch made earlier. Using three strands of thread, work each letter individually to avoid threads carried from one letter to another showing through.

4 To mount the finished work, cut a piece of wadding to 22 x 27cm (8 x 10in) and glue it to a piece of mounting card (available from art shops) cut to the same size. Fold the edges of the fabric over the card, ensuring the design is in the centre.

5 To secure in place, lace the fabric with strong thread, from top to bottom and side to side. Place in a picture frame (with or without glass) and add the back and strut. For this design we've used a 10in x 8in picture frame.

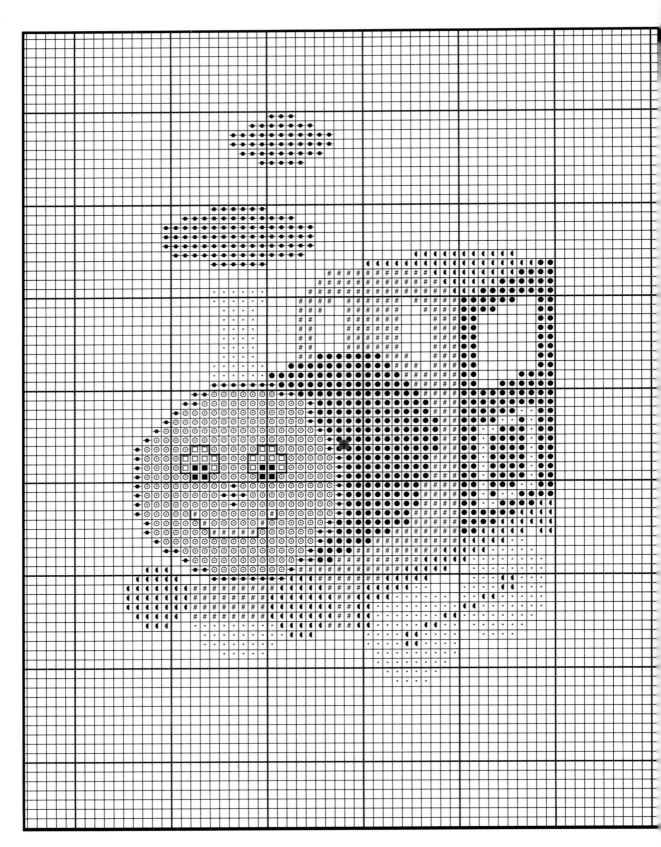

chapter 4
KITCHEN

JAR LACIES

Add a finishing touch to home-made preserves for the ideal gift.

STITCHING INSTRUCTIONS

KEY JAR LACIES

DMC	Anchor	Madeira		Colour
817	19	0211	■ ■	RED
9486	245	1404	× ×	GREEN
WHITE	1	WHITE	· ·	WHITE
444	290	0105	★ ★	YELLOW

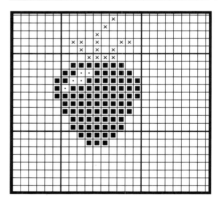

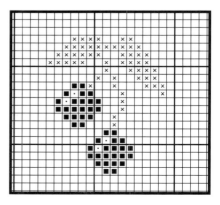

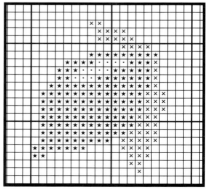

STITCHING THE JAR LACIES

1 Jar lacies add an attractive top to home made preserves as well as neatly identifying the flavouring. A printed check on plain weave cotton is ideal for cross stitching and practical for this project. Lace edging and 1cm wide ribbon adds a pretty finish. Using a 25cm (9in) square of fabric, mark a circle (using a plate or saucer) approximately 16cm (6³⁄₈in) in diameter. Next divide the circle into equal quarters with contrasting tacking thread.

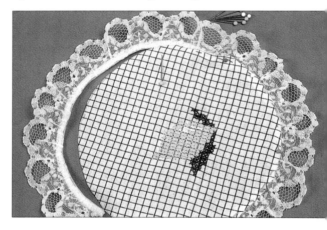

4 Trim the edge under approximately 0.4-0.5cm and pin the pre-gathered lace trim to the underside, over the turned edge. Work around the pot cover, until the lace ends meet. Overlap the lace edging approximately 1cm, turning the upper edge over so that the right side remains neat. Tack and then machine stitch the lace to the fabric all around the circumference.

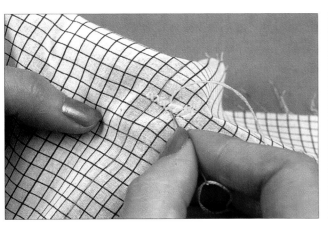

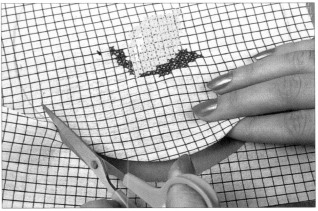

2 Using three strands of DMC stranded cotton, start each design – choose from lemon, strawberry or cherries. Stitch four cross stitches in each printed square and work in short rows to complete each design. When changing colours, fasten off and start again, rather than carry thread across the back of different coloured stitches, as this may show through and thus spoil the design.

3 Once the whole design is completed, trim around the edge of the circle along the outline previously drawn. It is advisable to use small, sharp embroidery scissors which will give greater control on small items and thus help achieve a neat circular edge.

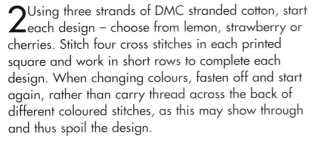

5 Place the finished cover over the jam pot and hold in place with a ribbon tie.

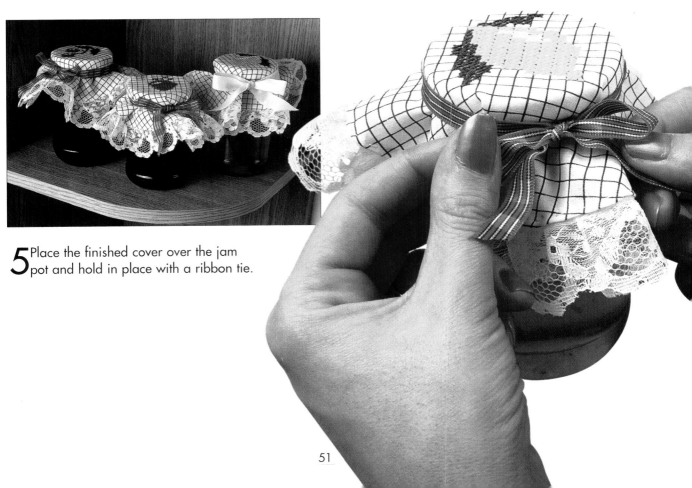

CAFE STYLE CURTAINS

How to add a continental feel to your kitchen.

STITCHING INSTRUCTIONS

KEY CAFE CURTAINS

DMC	Anchor	Madeira			Colour
700	228	1305	◆	◆	GREEN

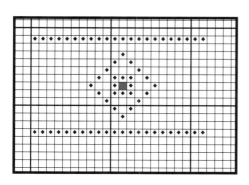

STITCHING THE CURTAINS

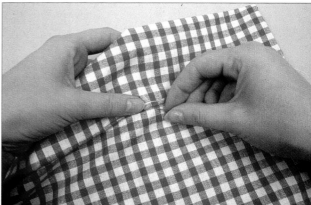

3 To finish the curtain, turn in side seams 1cm and again 1.5cm encasing raw edges. The cross stitch border should now be on the edge. Machine side seams. Press to form crisp edge. Turn up hem, leaving 2.5cm/1in (5 checks) between border and hemline. Turn raw edge under again and hem in place, using either hemming stitch or iron-on wondaweb.

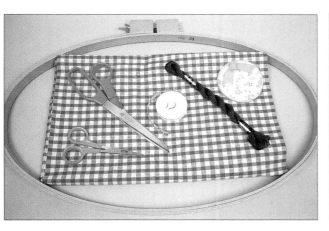

1 A cafe style curtain is particularly suited to gingham, an evenweave check fabric. Measure your window, adding 5cm (2in) to the width measure for side and seams, and select the depth required, again add an extra 6cm (2⅜in) for top seam and 10cm (4in) for deep hem. (Cafe curtains are usually hung halfway down the window.)

2 Using the embroidery hoop to hold the fabric taut whilst stitching, begin the design approximately 12.5cm (5in) from lower edge (19 checks) and 2.5cm (1in) from side (5 checks). Following the relevant charts from the chart section and using DMC cotton perle, work the borders in rows of cross stitch. Then stitch the motifs, working each stitch individually.

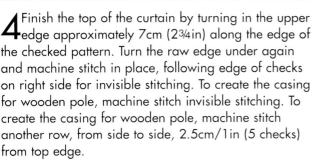

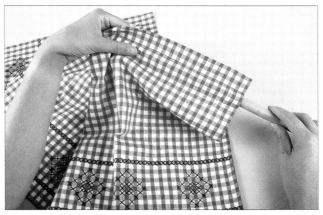

4 Finish the top of the curtain by turning in the upper edge approximately 7cm (2¾in) along the edge of the checked pattern. Turn the raw edge under again and machine stitch in place, following edge of checks on right side for invisible stitching. To create the casing for wooden pole, machine stitch invisible stitching. To create the casing for wooden pole, machine stitch another row, from side to side, 2.5cm/1in (5 checks) from top edge.

5 Cut a 1cm diameter wooden pole to the width of the window recess. Try it for size before inserting it between the top two rows of machine stitching. Adjust the curtain along the pole so that any gathers are even.

NAPKIN RINGS

This geometric design can be used to enhance a variety of tablewear - adding an individual touch to every meal.

STITCHING INSTRUCTIONS

KEY NAPKIN RINGS

DMC	Anchor	Madeira		Colour
700	228	1305	◆ ◆	GREEN

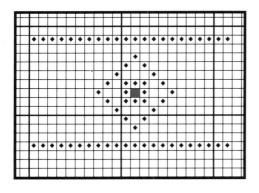

MAKING THE NAPKIN RINGS

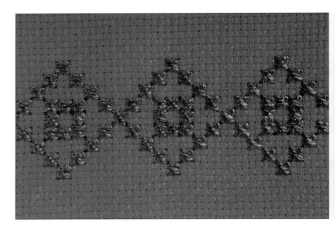

1 Cut a strip of 14 HPI aida approximately 6cm wide x 17cm (2½ x 6¾in) long. Starting 1cm from one of the short edges, start the design (following the chart) and using DMC cotton perle. Work each cross of the stitch over 2 holes of the aida and stitch each cross stitch individually.

4 With right sides facing, pin short ends of aida and gingham together to form a ring, matching motifs. Machine stitch and then press the seam edges open.

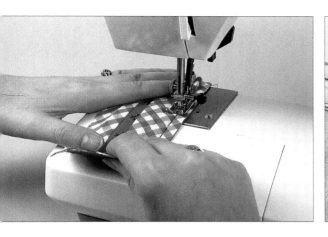

2 Repeat the motif along the strip of aida, using one point stitch as a common stitch for two motifs. Cut two strips of gingham on the bias, approximately 3cm (1½in) wide and 17cm (6¾in) long. With right sides together, machine stitch one piece to the aida along the top approximately 1cm from edge. Repeat for lower edge.

3 Fold the gingham back along the stitching so right sides show, press for crisp firm edge. Repeat on lower edge. Turn in again, encasing raw edges and press, do not sew. Open out gingham.

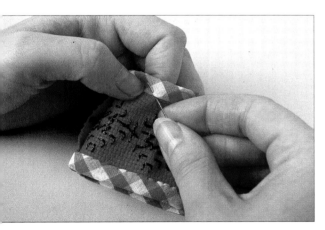

5 Finally, working from the wrong side, fold the gingham bias strips over the raw edges of top and bottom of the napkin ring and slip stitch to the aida.

MATCHING NAPKIN

An inexpensive way to co-ordinate stitching designs for your tablewear.

STITCHING INSTRUCTIONS

KEY MATCHING NAPKIN

DMC	Anchor	Madeira		Colour
700	228	1305	◆ ◆	GREEN

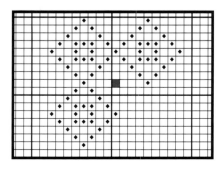

MAKING THE NAPKIN

1 Cut two triangular pieces of red aida, each approximately 11 x 11 x 15.5cm (4 x 4 x 6in) with which to make the corner decorative pieces for the napkins. Starting at the short point, approximately 2cm from edge, begin the diamond cross stitch design.

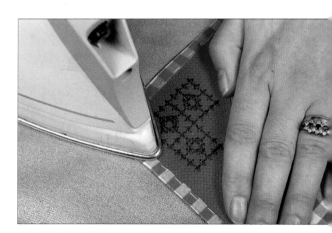

4 Fold in the gingham edge approximately 0.5cm around the whole napkin and then again to encase the raw edge and edge of decorative corner pieces. Tack in place and gently press to hold edges before stitching.

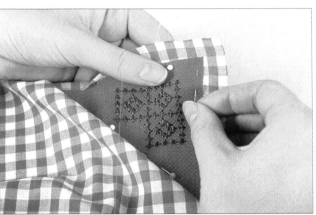

2 Continue cross stitching the motif, so that the left and right edges of the first diamond form part of the next two diamonds. Cut the napkins from gingham, approximately 34cm (13½in) square.

3 Turn in 0.5cm of the lower (longest) edge of the cross stitched aid triangles, tack in place and press firmly with a warm iron. Pin and tack the triangles to two opposite corners of napkin, leaving approximately 1cm of gingham edge to fold back over as edging.

5 Carefully machine stitch the turned in edge all around the napkin to neaten edges. Also stitch across the outer edge of the aida triangle to the napkin. Remove tacking stitches. Press firmly with a damp press cloth and hot iron. The napkin is now ready to slip into the napkin ring.

POT HOLDER

Protect your hands with this practical cloth - which will also look cheery when hung up beside the oven.

STITCHING INSTRUCTIONS

KEY POT HOLDER

DMC	Anchor	Madeira		Colour
700	228	1305	◆ ◆	GREEN

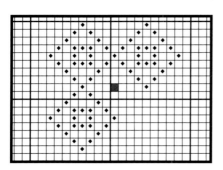

MAKING THE POT HOLDER

3 Pin the padded backing to the aida, wrong sides together. Tack and stitch in place. Cut strips of gingham on the bias, approximately 2.5cm (1in) wide. Join together to form one strip 68cm (26½in) long. Starting at one corner, pin one edge of the strip to the aida side of the pot holder. Tack in place, turning at the corners.

1 Cut a piece of aida approximately 17cm (6¾in) square to make the pot holder. Starting in the centre of the piece, cross stitch the design, repeating the diamond pattern four times (see the chart on page 54). Add a single cross stitch in the centre to complete the pattern.

2 Cut a piece of gingham and a piece of 0.5cm thick wadding the same size as the aida, approximately 17cm (6¾in) square. Attach the wadding and gingham to form the heat resistant backing, by machine stitching the two fabrics together at approximately 2.5cm (1in) intervals.

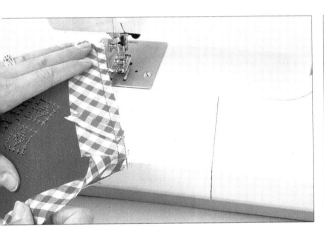

4 Make a loop from gingham approximately 9 x 2.5cm (3½ x 1in). Stitch the long edge, turn through and press. Attach the loop to one corner of the pad, slipping ends under the gingham trim. Machine stitch the trim to the pad, including loop ends.

5 Once all sides have been machine stitched, press using a dry press cloth. Fold the trim over along the stitching. Fold over again to encase raw edges and then turn under the trim edge and slip stitch to the back of the pad.

KITCHEN ROLLER BLIND

A fresh decorative finish for an everyday blind.

STITCHING INSTRUCTIONS

KEY KITCHEN BLIND

DMC	Anchor	Madeira			Colour
700	228	1305	◆	◆	GREEN

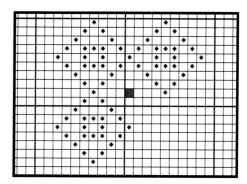

STITCHING THE ROLLER BLIND

1 Measure the window recess accurately in order to determine width and length of the blind. Ensure the fabric chosen is at least 5cm (2in) wider and 20cm (7in) longer than the recess to allow for hems. Cut a length of gingham for the trim approximately 20cm (7in) wide.

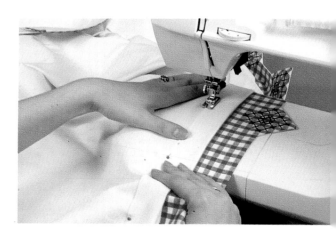

4 Turn work to the right sides, press firmly for crisp edge. Next, pin, tack and stitch the main fabric for the blind to the top of the edge of the trim, right sides together. Open out and press to form a crisp edge. Working on the right side, again machine stitch through all thicknesses approximately 3cm (1¼in) from edge to form the pocket for the blind lath.

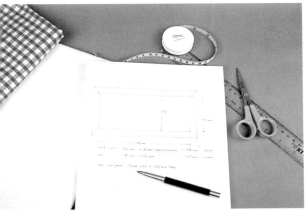

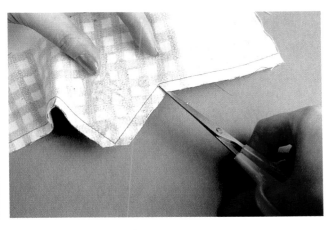

2 Starting at the centre of the gingham, cross stitch the diamond design. Repeat the design either side f the centre diamond, leaving 7 gingham checks etween each design.

3 Stiffen the gingham trim by ironing fusible interfacing on the wrong side. Leave to cool. Pin and tack a piece of the main fabric, approximately 14cm (5½in) wide, to the trim, with right sides together. Machine stitch, starting at one edge level with the centre of the cross stitch diamonds. Stitch around each design, pivoting at the bottom. Trim seam allowance and clip corners.

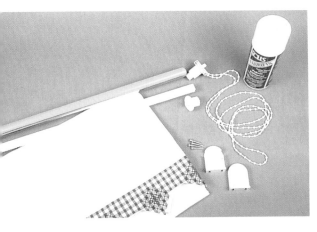

5 Hem each side of the blind by turning in approximately 2.5cm (1in) either side and machine stitching. (The fabric width should be 1.2cm ess than the blind roller width.) Neaten raw edges of he top by overstitching or turning under the hemming. Spray with fabric stiffener and attach to a purchased olind kit following manufacturer's instructions.

TEATIME TRAY CLOTH

Complement this tea tray cloth with this versatile design.

STITCHING INSTRUCTIONS

KEY TRAY CLOTH

DMC	Anchor	Madeira			Colour
700	228	1305	◆	◆	GREEN

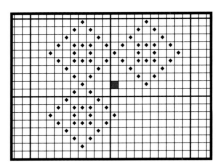

STITCHING THE TRAY CLOTH

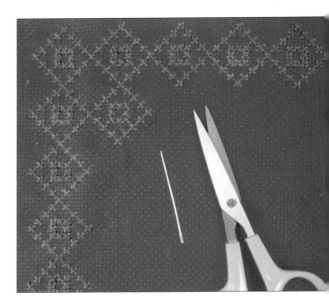

1 Cut pieces of 14HPI aida and gingham to fit the tea tray. Work the design in one corner of the aida, approximately 3.5cm (1⅜in) from the edge. Cross stitch 5 diamonds along one edge. At right angles to the first row, work another 4 diamonds and to finish, add another diamond at the corner.

4 Fold the binding again to encase the raw edges of the tray cloth. Turn under the remaining raw edge of the binding strip and then slip stitch to the underside of the tray cloth. Press again, using a damp press cloth and hot iron.

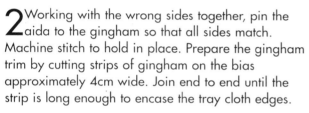

2 Working with the wrong sides together, pin the aida to the gingham so that all sides match. Machine stitch to hold in place. Prepare the gingham trim by cutting strips of gingham on the bias approximately 4cm wide. Join end to end until the strip is long enough to encase the tray cloth edges.

3 Start at one corner and working with right sides together, pin, tack and then machine stitch the gingham binding to the tray cloth, turning at corners. Trim seam allowances to a scant 0.5cm all around. Fold binding back along stitching line. Press.

TIMELY TEA COSY

Complete the linen set by stitching this stylish teapot cosy.

KEY TEA COSY

DMC	Anchor	Madeira			Colour
700	228	1305	◆	◆	GREEN

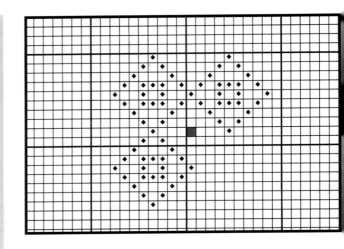

MAKING THE TEA COSY

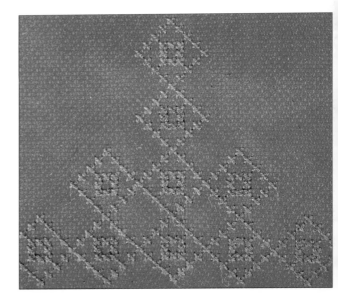

1 Cut a piece of aida approximately 28 x 34cm (11 x 13in). Starting at the centre, approximately 3cm (1¼in) from the lower edge, cross stitch the first diamond, using DMC cotton perle. Repeat the design, working four diamonds each side of the centre, joining the diamonds using one side stitch as a common stitch between diamonds.

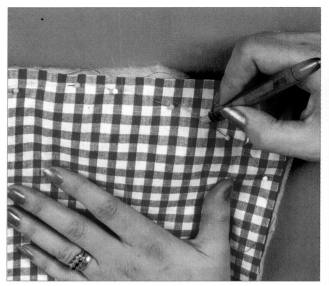

2 Once the design is complete, sandwich the aida between wadding and gingham, with right side facing the gingham. Mark the tea cosy shape onto the gingham, starting at the centre. Machine stitch the bottom edge only. Make the back of the tea cosy in the same way. Trim stitched edges to within 0.5cm of stitching, turn to encase wadding.

3 Next, pin the three layers together and machine stitch around remaining edges. Pin both front and back together, matching stitching lines, and with right sides showing. Tack in place. Add the gingham binding by cutting strips of gingham on the bias approximately 3.5cm (1⅜in) wide. Join together to create a length that will encase cosy edges. Tack one edge to the right side of the cosy, over the stitching lines.

TIP:
To make a loop, cut a strip approximately 4cm (1½in) long x 3.5cm (1⅜in) wide. Stitch long edges together, turn and press. Add to cosy at the same time as the binding.

5 Fold the binding over to the back, encasing the edges. Turn remaining raw edge under again and pin to back of cosy. Slip stitch in place to finish, also encasing the other loop end at the top of the cosy.

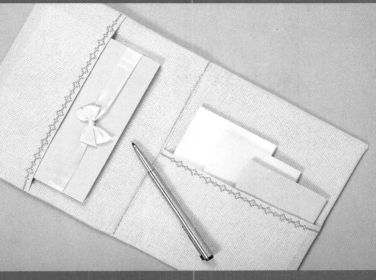

chapter 5
GIFTS

GIFT TAGS

STITCHING INSTRUCTIONS

KEY GIFT TAGS

DMC	Anchor	Madeira		Colour
797	123	0912	× ×	BLUE
352	9	0303	O O	PEACH
905	258	1413	ς ς	GREEN
760	895	0813	● ●	PINK
562	205	1213	# #	GREEN

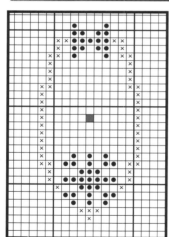

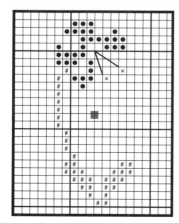

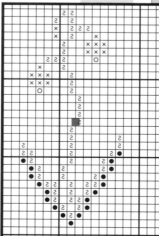

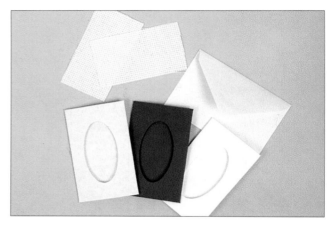

1 Personalised gift tags add a very individual touch to any present, either as a finishing touch to a handcrafted gift or a more personal feel on a purchased one. Select suitable gift cards with cut outs, readily available from art/craft shops. Cut 11HPI pearl aida approximately 3cm (1¼in) larger than card size to allow for handling.

4 Centre the design, right side down, over the hole, using the left flap as backing. Trim away any excess aida that overlaps the card edge. Carefully open card, holding design in place on left flap now right side up. Gently lift edges and glue or tape in place to hold securely.

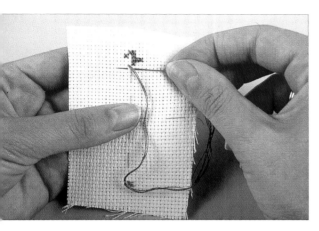

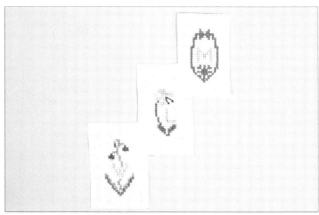

2 Tack around the design area and then choose the design and initial (chosen from the alphabet chart on page 10) suitable for the occasion. Mark the centre of the design area with tacking thread. Using three strands of stranded cotton, either start at the top or at the centre, working each stitch separately.

3 Continue working the design, following the chart and counting holes and stitches to ensure the spacing is accurate. Once the motif and initial has been completed, gently press the pieces, using a soft towel surface and dry press cloth. Once cool, trim to approximately 0.5cm smaller than the card size.

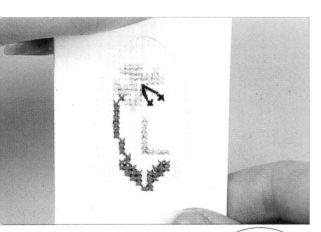

5 If using glue, wait until it has dried before the next application. Alternatively, use double-sided tape around the edges of the card and cut out. Fold the left flap over the window and press firmly around the edges to secure.

TIP
Extra pressing between books can help to secure the card and design in place if glue is reluctant to hold.

WRITING CASE AND SPECTACLES CASE

STITCHING INSTRUCTIONS

KEY BOTH CASES

DMC	Anchor	Madeira			Colour
3689	74	0607	■	■	PINK
3803	65	0602	★	★	BIRGUNDY

MAKING THE WRITING CASE

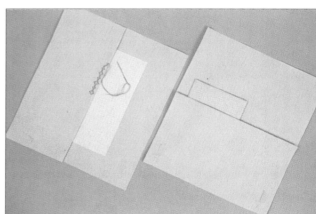

1 Again using a firm 11HPI canvas to provide some support, cut the canvas to the desired size, approximately 25cm wide x 30cm (9 x 11in). Using a pencil, mark the outer edge of the front panel, approximately 20 x 23cm (7 x 9in). Mark a central line from top to bottom and then mark the placement lines for the wording. Three lines have been used in this project, each separated by two squares with each letter standing 7 squares high. (Use the alphabet chart on page 11 to select wording.)

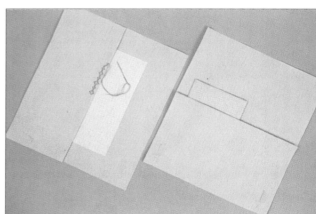

4 Cut the lining pieces from 14 HPI grey fabric, adding two half size pieces for stationery pockets. Turn in 1cm on inner edge of pockets and press firmly with steam iron. Cross stitch the inner border pattern from the cover, holding the turned edge in place. Machine stitch the pockets in place, leaving the decorative edge free.

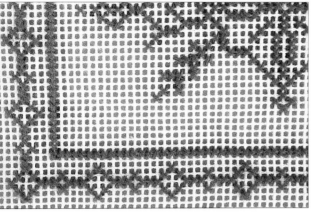

2 Calculate the word spacing by counting number of stitches and spaces in each letter/word. Halve the total in each line and count back from the centre to find starting point. Then using one strand of 3-ply yarn, cross stitch the chosen wording. Next, stitch around the marked border, using the dark rose yarn to match the lettering and following the chart.

TIP
If desired, repeat the front design, without wording, for the back cover of the case.

3 Work the motif in the centre, five rows from the border. Then fill in the centre panel with one strand of pink 3 ply yarn. Stitch the letters and outer edge of main motif and in the centre of the border motif. Finish the design with contrasting soft grey to completely fill the motif and outer edge of the case.

5 Machine stitch the outer front piece to the inside front and outer back to inside back, working with right sides together. Leave open at spine. Turn to right sides and press gently. Insert card, cut to size, between the two layers of front and back. Turn in the spine edges to neaten and slip stitch the back to front to form the case.

WRITING CASE AND SPECTACLES CASE CONTINUED.

Using the same chart and key as the writing case (on the previous page no. 71).

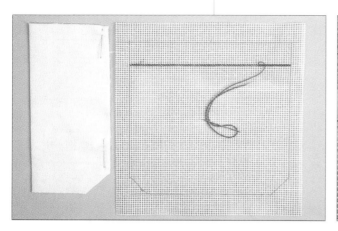

1 To provide reasonable protection, we have used a firm 11HPI canvas for the spectacles case. Cut the canvas to approximately 21cm wide x 22cm (8¼ x 8¾ in) and then mark the outline of the case with a pencil. Begin the first row of the cross stitch design, using one strand of 3-ply wool and following the chart.

2 Continue to fill in the design on both sides of the case, completing the motif outline in the darker thread, before adding the pale pink and soft grey stitches. Once complete, prepare the case lining, cut from cotton poplin. Cut the lining to the same size as the canvas outline.

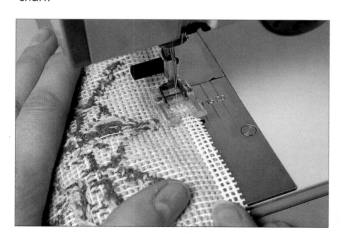

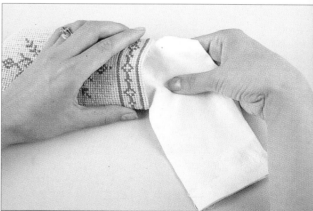

3 Fold the lining in half and machine stitch around the shaped ends and side seam. Press well. Working with right sides together, fold the completed canvas in half and machine stitch the shaped end and side. Turn to right sides and press gently, using a dry press cloth and warm iron.

4 Fit the lining into the case so that seams match and the wrong sides of lining and case are together. Turn in the top opening of both case and lining by approximately 1cm.

chapter 6

CARDS

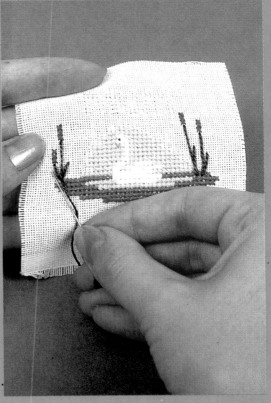

HAPPY BIRTHDAY CARDS

Personalised cards that will make lasting impressions.

STITCHING INSTRUCTIONS

KEY BIRTHDAY CARDS

DMC	Anchor	Madeira		Colour
CAR				
666	9046	0510	# #	RED
928	1708	3948	♥ ♥	PALE GREY
310	403	BLACK	■ ■	BLACK
444	291	0105	⊙ ⊙	YELLOW
SWAN				
3826	349	2009	○ ○	BROWN
966	203	1209	J J	GREEN
825	147	0912	# #	BRIGHT BLUE
3761	160	0908	⊙ ⊙	PALE BLUE
977	304	0203	◆ ◆	ORANGE
310	403	BLACK	● ●	BLACK
WHITE	1	WHITE	□ □	WHITE

STITCHING THE CARDS

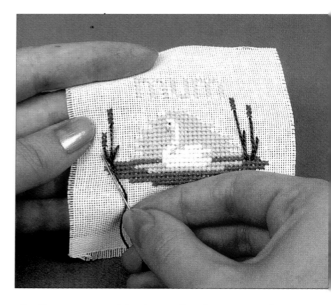

1 Choose a suitable design for the person; these projects show a swan among bullrushes for Mum and a colourful car for Dad. Cross stitch the design (following the relevant charts), onto a piece of 11HPI aida approximately 2cm larger than the card window.

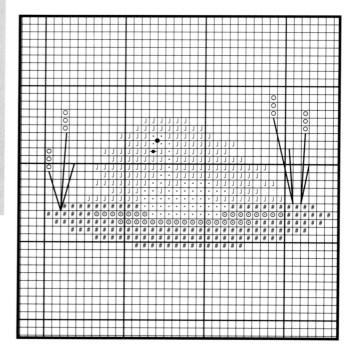

2 Position the completed design over the cut-out hole of the card and gently mark the corners on the wrong side. Trim away any excess fabric, leaving approximately 1cm all around to attach to the card.

3 Again, position the design over the hole, making sure it is central and square within the window. Dab a little glue to each corner to hold in place before adding strips of glue to the left hand flap and along the design edges. Close the flap over the design and press firmly together.

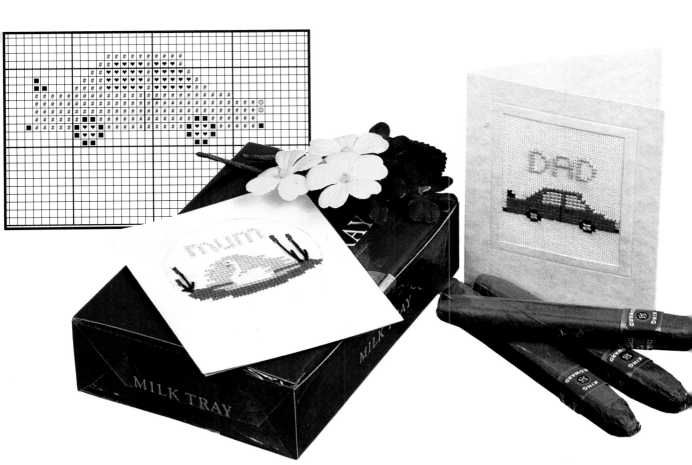

CHRISTMAS CARDS AND TAGS

Stitch a festive card and gift tag to add that finishing touch to your presents.

STITCHING INSTRUCTIONS

DMC	Anchor	Madeira		Colour
666	9046	0510	# #	RED
986	246	1314	♥ ♥	DARK GREEN
444	290	0105	● ●	YELLOW
648	398	1902	○ ○	GREY

KEY CHRISTMAS CARDS

MAKING THE CARDS

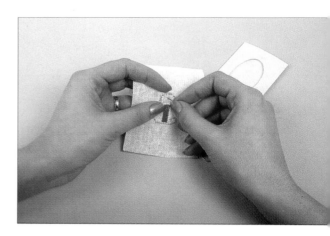

1 Cut a piece of 11HPI aida approximately the same size as the folded card. Mark the centre of the fabric with running stitches in order to position the design. Stitch the chosen festive message by following the charts, using three strands of embroidery thread.

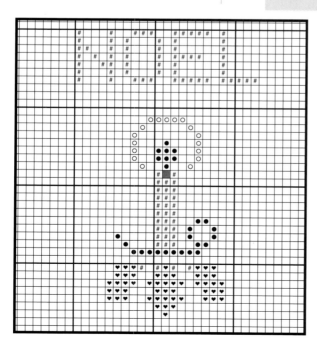

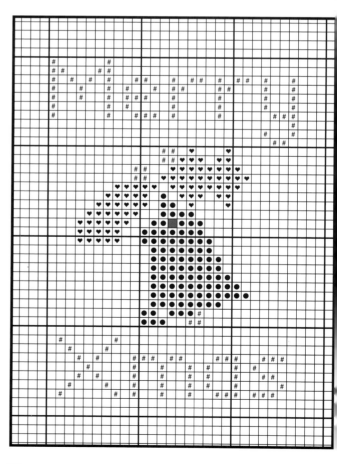

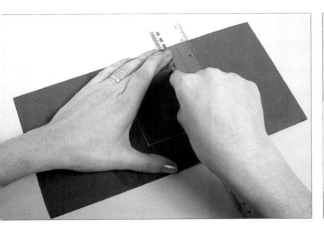

2 To make your own cards, cut a piece of card (available from art shops) 30 x 15cm (11 x 6in). Gently score two fold lines 10cm apart and fold both in to the centre. On the centre panel, mark the window area approximately 6 x 8cm (2 x 3in) starting 3cm (1¼in) from the top edge and 4cm from the bottom edge. Carefully draw a border approximately 0.3cm from the pencilled edge, using a contrasting colour, before cutting out the window.

3 Place the completed design over the cut-out, leaving a selvage for gluing, trim away any excess fabric. Dab glue on to each corner and press firmly to hold in place. Add strips of glue around the sides of the left flap of the card, plus strips along the outer edge of the aida. Close the flap over the design and press together, leaving under a weight to dry.

SPECIAL OCCASION CARDS

Make a unique card to commemorate a special occasion.

STITCHING INSTRUCTIONS

MAKING THE CARDS

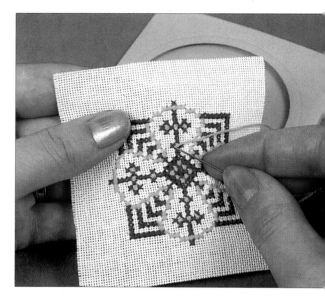

1 Whether for moving to a new home or as a simple thank you, an individually stitched card can become a treasured memento. Cut a small piece of 11HPI aida approximately 2cm larger than the folded card size. Following the charts and using three strands of embroidery thread, complete each design in the centre of the aida.

KEY COTTAGE CARD

DMC	Anchor	Madeira			Colour
995	410	1102	◖	◖	ELECTRIC BLUE
3827	363	2209	◄	◄	LIGHT TAN
775	976	1001	●	●	DARK BLUE
349	13	0212	·	·	RED
701	227	1305	★	★	FERN GREEN
420	370	2214	⊙	⊙	BROWN
310	403	BLACK	╕	╕	BLACK

KEY SNOWFLAKE CARD

DMC	Anchor	Madeira			Colour
791	149	0914	●	●	DARK BLUE
747	928	1104	×	×	LIGHT BLUE

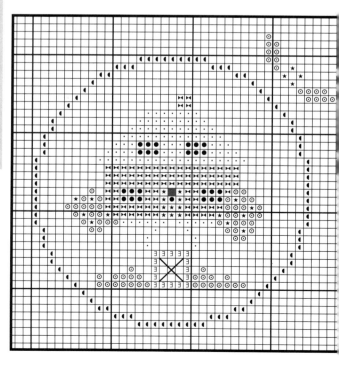

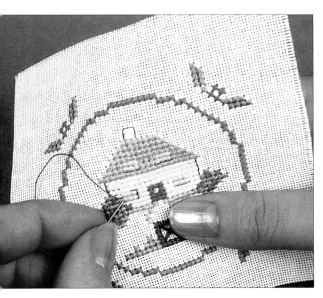

2 To emphasise particular areas, such as the chimney or window frames of the house, use a single strand of embroidery thread and simple back stitch to outline the feature desired. Then place the finished piece over the cut out hole, pencil mark four points around the edge and trim away excess aida, leaving a border approximately 1cm all around.

3 Place trimmed piece over the window, face down and whilst holding in place, lift each of the corners and add a dab of glue to hold securely. Using double sided tape (or glue), tape around all edges of the left flap of card as well as along the edges of the aida. Close the flap over the design and press firmly in place.

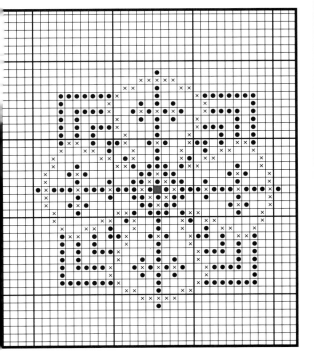

ACKNOWLEDGEMENTS

Stranded Cotton
Aida and Damask Linen - DMC Creative World Ltd
Anchor Embroidery thread - Coats Leisure Crafts Group

BIBLIOGRAPHY

Cross Stitch Designs – Kate Greenaway (David & Charles)
Cross Stitch Design Manual – Fran Rose (David & Charles)
The Cross Stitch and Sampler Book – Liz Mundle and John Eaton
(Apple Press)